PUTTING THE HEART IN YOUR HOME   BY Jean Lemmon

MEREDITH® BOOKS   DES MOINES, IOWA

PUTTING THE HEART IN YOUR HOME
by Jean LemMon
Editor: Vicki Ingham
Design: The Design Office of Jerry J. Rank
Copy Chief: Terri Fredrickson
Copy and Production Editor: Victoria Forlini
Editorial Operations Manager: Karen Schirm
Managers, Book Production: Pam Kvitne, Marjorie J. Schenkelberg, Rick von Holdt
Contributing Copy Editor: Lori Blachford
Contributing Proofreaders: Sue Fetters, Beth Havey, Nancy Ruhling
Indexer: Stephanie J. Reymann
Editorial and Design Assistants: Kaye Chabot, Karen McFadden, Mary Lee Gavin

MEREDITH® BOOKS
Editor in Chief: Linda Raglan Cunningham
Design Director: Matt Strelecki
Executive Editor, Home Decorating and Design: Denise L. Caringer

Publisher: James D. Blume
Executive Director, Marketing: Jeffrey Myers
Executive Director, New Business Development: Todd M. Davis
Executive Director, Sales: Ken Zagor
Director, Operations: George A. Susral
Director, Production: Douglas M. Johnston
Business Director: Jim Leonard

Vice President and General Manager: Douglas J. Guendel

MEREDITH PUBLISHING GROUP
President, Publishing Group: Stephen M. Lacy
Vice President-Publishing Director: Bob Mate

MEREDITH CORPORATION
Chairman and Chief Executive Officer: William T. Kerr

In Memoriam: E. T. Meredith III (1933-2003)

COVER PHOTOGRAPH: Copyright The Estate of Barbra Walz

All of us at Meredith® Books are dedicated to providing you with information and ideas to enhance your home. We welcome your comments and suggestions.
Write to us at: Better Homes and Gardens Books, Home Decorating and Design Editorial Department, 1716 Locust St., Des Moines, IA 50309-3023.

If you would like to purchase any of our home decorating and design, cooking, crafts, gardening, or home improvement books,
check wherever quality books are sold. Or visit us at: meredithbooks.com

homes are a heart-to-heart thing with me.

When I think back, I realize I've had a serious love affair with every home I've lived in! With some houses it was love at first sight. Others needed enhancements before true affection set in. Either way, each house or apartment has charmed me, embraced me, and provided the perfect ambience for who I am and how I want to live.

My current home, a 1941 bungalow that looks like a little red barn in the woods, thrilled me to the depths of my soul the moment I walked in with the real estate agent. There was something about the spaces, the architectural oddities, and the way the light came through the windows that seemed to scream "The Forties"—so much so that I could have sworn I heard faint echoes of Big Band music. I fell in love with this house instantly and completely.

But before this latest love, there were other houses and, of course, the working woman's veritable parade of apartments with Murphy beds, sofa beds, and 20-inch ranges that never seemed to have working ovens. Even those apartments, however, were love affairs because I was allowed to give them my own stamp. Only part of the magic in my relationship

with these places came from the structure itself. THE REST CAME FROM THE DECORATING.

My first apartment in Des Moines always will be one of my favorites. At first glance it was just a cramped, blah-looking studio apartment on the second floor of an old frame home, but immediately I saw its potential.

It had great woodwork and nice windows, including a little bay. And it felt like a tree house snuggled into the branches of the soaring oaks that surrounded it. Those attributes more than offset the sofa bed and the refrigerator-size bath with a shower that only trickled water—usually not as warm as I would have liked.

The other good thing about that apartment was the landlord. He seemed pleased that I wanted to paint, add new window treatments, and eventually replace the apartment's standard-issue furniture with some of my own. THE PLACE WOULD HAVE CHARACTER—MY CHARACTER.

The transformation started with a lighter paint color that made the space look less confining. The color also created a lively, happy feeling that matched and expressed my enthusiasm for a new city and an exciting new job as a junior editor at *Better Homes and Gardens* magazine.

After the color change came breezy window treatments and, one by one, pieces of furniture chosen for their uniqueness and because I loved them. I must confess that after 40 years, I still have many of those pieces. And I still love them. They always manage to fit in wherever I live.

"I'm convinced homes can be designed to make their occupants feel complete and satisfied."

Through the years I've learned to create home environments that nurture my emotional side and my lifestyle. I've accomplished the same thing for design clients and on the pages of various magazines. And I'm convinced homes can be designed to make the people who live in them feel complete and satisfied, no matter what their prevailing interests or

attitudes. Call it the American version of feng shui—the home reflects the spirit of its owners.

I've always believed HOMES SHOULD BE MORE THAN VISUALLY PLEASING. They also should BE EMOTIONALLY SATISFYING. They should wrap their arms around you, give you comfort, support your interests, match your mood, and mirror your personality.

In this book I'll help you discover the special tricks and touches that can turn standard design elements into emotional and psychological tools. That's the secret—and the bottom line—to creating a "feel-good" home.

A home is meant to be loved. And your home should also MAKE YOU FEEL LOVED!

Jean LemMon

Former Editor in Chief,
Better Homes and Gardens magazine

MY PLACE: WHERE I HANG MY HAT AND HEART

security
simplicity
whimsy
happiness
romance
serenity
comfort
escapes
enrichment
celebration

Baby
Bear

Father Bear

Mother Bea

my place

When visiting with readers over the years, I often heard one question asked over and over. "What does your home look like?" In response (and with more truth than modesty) I've had to admit, "Well, it's certainly not as impressive as many of the homes we've featured in *Better Homes and Gardens* magazine." And that about sums it up.

I didn't choose my home—or decorate it—to be a showplace. Rather, I wanted it to **nurture** my emotions, to match my varied moods and interests. My home does just that. It's unpretentious and comfortable. It harbors enough **tradition** and pieces of my past to anchor me in a

frenetic present. It connects me with **nature** visually and physically and like a warm smile at the front door, it's friendly and welcoming.

If there's a secret ingredient to my decorating style, **IT'S LOVE.** Everything in my home is there because I love it, not necessarily because it's fashionable or because I need it. And while love is the underlying impetus in my decorating, my home encompasses many other **emotional qualities.** I'm sure all of our homes do, because none of us is one-dimensional. I'm certain a person who wants a decorating look that offers "serenity" also can want a wisp of "whimsy" or a whisper of "romance." To show you what I mean, come with me and let's take a quick tour of my home.

My living room is my **"enrichment"** area. It's here I read by the fireside, relax at the piano, or paint in a sunny spot by the window. In this room the focal point is not the bookcase-flanked fireplace, but the undecorated window that overlooks a wooded ravine. The tiny den just off the living room is my unwind-and-put-my-feet-up **"comfort"** area. It's my favorite place to lounge on the sofa and watch old movies or the birds and squirrels outside the window.

The dining room is my **"celebration"** room—the place where I celebrate good times with special people. It's also a room that celebrates heritage. This is where I set the table using Mom's Sunday best dishes and where I feel the embrace of generations of family in a collection of memorabilia.

"WHIMSY" takes over in my kitchen eating area. It's a breezy, lighthearted spot, where my puppy and I enjoy breakfast and I read the paper to the accompaniment of scampering furry feet and the squeaking of pet toys. And my petite side patio is pure "escape." It's beautifully peaceful, nestled next to my backyard garden, and it gives me the snug, smug feeling of having found a secret place all my own.

So there you have it—the little cottage I live in. Like its predecessors, it exhibits DOWN-HOME comfort, warmth, and a relaxed livability. (Those same characteristics, incidentally, also define my daughter's home, which you'll see on pages 30–31.) Home to home—generation to generation—in this family, comfort and warmth are our keys to decorating success.

What does my home look like? Maybe it looks like lots of other modest, nicely furnished cottages. Maybe it only looks like me. However it might be judged, it's the most COMFORTABLE place I know and I enjoy every minute in it. It's home—my place—where I hang my HAT AND HEART!

PAGE 17: My kindergarten teacher thought this crayon drawing was worth saving. So Mom did. PAGES 19, 20: My living room harbors my FAVORITE TOYS— my piano and easel—set up in a SUNNY CORNER by the window. The piano top also is a gallery of family photos—my homesteading grandmother, Mom as a child, and Dad as a young man about town. OPPOSITE: This room suits me to a tee. It's where I read (sitting in the wing chair or lounging on the sofa), entertain, and ENJOY the antiques I've accumulated over the years—the pine hutch, a collection of primitive benches, a pair of burned-wood side tables, and even my folks' old curlicued floor lamp.

Designed to be as comforting as a hug."

a CROCHET THROW and a Norwegian hardanger tablecloth, *opposite*, remind me of generations of family needleworkers, although these are antique shop finds. The pint-size piano, another antique, has been commandeered by my toddler grandson. We play duets. Sort of. The little den off the living room, *above*, is where my family and friends gravitate for coffee or drinks. For a coffee table I've used a carpenter's toolbox, which stores outdoor cushions when they're not in use. The wall shelf, carved by a regional craftsman, substitutes for a mantel, and the watercolor was painted by an artist from my first hometown—Duluth.

DINING IS ALWAYS A PLEASURE no matter how fancy or simple the meal. I love this room because of its special-to-me accessories. Here the mantel clock my grandfather ordered from a catalog and a photo of my grandmother in a carved frame she brought from Norway are displayed with Father Christmases made for me by a wood-carver friend. And the table is often set with some of my collection of Redwing pottery.

NOTHING IS EVER VERY SERIOUS in my breakfast area, *above*. To underscore that, a rabbit-themed rug hangs on the wall to give the room a dose of whimsy while establishing its color scheme. **MORNING COFFEE** always tastes better on my tiny side patio, *opposite*. This is my escape place when life gets frantic. And it's so simple—an inexpensive bistro set, a couple of primitive benches, and some potted plants.

STYLE SEEMS TO BE HEREDITARY—at least in our family. The cottage my daughter Becky has decorated for herself, husband Bill, and son Noah has definite traces of my style. (Of course the fact that she shops my basement for no-longer-in-use items helps the look along.) Both of us are devotees of comfortable living, but Becky has to add a level of practicality and indestructibility. Hence the slipcovers for sofa and chair. In its summer "dress," *below*, the living room is light and monochromatic with only touches of blue in the quilt's border and the throw pillows. For winter, *opposite*, Becky warms up the room with a red and white quilt and a red and creamy white toile slipcover on the sofa. The chair retains the beige checked slipcover that works well for both seasons, while the chair's throw and the sofa's pillows switch to warm brick red. The prize in her burgeoning collection of pyrographic pieces is the room's coffee table, which weathers all seasons.

"LIKE MOTHER...
LIKE DAUGHTER."

security

simplicity
whimsy
happiness
romance
serenity
comfort
escapes
enrichment
celebration

security

In a world that's more than a little scary at times, the need to feel loved, secure, and protected is fast becoming one of our "BASIC HUMAN NEEDS"—right up there with air, water, food, and shelter.

If anyone were to ask what would make me feel most secure, I'd have to answer: "being constantly surrounded by people who love me." Great! But impossible!

Next best thing? Being surrounded by walls that because of their color or pattern ENGULF AND COMFORT ME; deep, luxurious cushions that I can sink into; and at the end of a day, a comfortable bed loaded

with soft pillows and a sinfully luscious down comforter that I can snuggle in under.

MY HOME IS MY SAFE HAVEN—the spot where I can shed the world and feel protected. Every place I've lived has played that role in my life, starting with my folks' small farmhouse. And it was during those early years, living in a house my parents had built themselves, that I learned how well HOMES CAN NURTURE AND COMFORT their inhabitants.

Saturday mornings at home were wonderful, happy times. I'd help Mom clean our house, although (not being thrilled at having been appointed chief duster) I hated dusting the curlicues on the old metal floor lamp. That lamp is now in my own living room, and I'm still not fond of dusting it. BUT I LOVE IT—AND THE memories that come bubbling up every time I turn it on.

I know now that it was because of years of Saturday morning dusting sessions that I began to notice and CARE ABOUT THOSE THINGS THAT MADE OUR HOME LOOK AND FEEL so cozy, lived in, and loved. It was many years later that I learned the decorating skills needed to pull all those elements together—not just dust them!

There's nothing like a sloped ceiling to bring a room RIGHT UP CLOSE around you. And the squat little window only accentuates the area's protective, umbrella-like quality. To keep a room like this from feeling claustrophobic, limit furnishings to a muted monochromatic range, such as blues, gray, and white. Although the coloration of the room is subtle, visual interest comes from the MIX OF PATTERNS AND TEXTURES, including pillows of ticking stripes, checks, and quilt blocks, all topping a heritage quilt. The result is a room as far away from the cares of the world as a bear cub's den.

THE GOAL a room that's
as comfortable
as your OLD SLIPPers.

SPACE can work for you or against you in creating a room that feels snug and cocoonlike. To the person who craves a cozy environment, a room that's bigger is not always better. Rooms—like shoes—can be just as uncomfortable if they're too big or too small.

Naturally a small space is easier to draw in around you; but if you've been dealt a cavern-size room, there are ways to tame it and give it a more intimate atmosphere. Adding beams to a high ceiling or painting it a darker color are two ways to keep a room's emotional warmth from escaping through a lofty ceiling. An even easier fix is to subdivide the oversize area by creating several smaller furniture groupings within it or by parceling off sections of the room with floor-standing dividers.

Of course, lower ceilings are easier to work with than high ceilings when you're making a room wrap you like your favorite sweater. The

IF a room could be a woolly sweater, THIS one would! The tiny space is filled with small-scale furniture—lots of it. Filling the corner with a folding screen, adding a desk under the window, and pulling up a tall bench anchored by a rug create a snug little getaway. A more than generous helping of accessories and several powerful patterns add to the room's cuddly quality. The secret ingredient is an attractively overcrowded furniture arrangement.

If this room were empty, it would make a great dance hall. So all the room-snugging ploys have been called into play to make the space homey and inviting. To start with, beams are added to visually lower the ceiling. Then two more design devices make the ceiling seem lower and closer than it actually is—a wainscot treatment that reaches up nearly to the top of the door frames and a darker tone of paint on the wall above it. Several small furniture groupings, each defined by an area rug, and the warming addition of wood, stone, and a Franklin stove rein in the untamed space and create a cozy nest.

Goldilocks really could have gotten lost in these chairs! The mismatched pair of hefty wing chairs fills one end of this small room. And when you team them with a sofa facing the fireplace, you're surrounded by a furniture grouping that makes you want to snuggle in beside the fire and enjoy a cup of tea. Other elements that, because of their height, add to the PROTECTIVE FEELING of this area are the taller-than-usual side table and the wall-hugging chest of drawers. While the upholstered pieces are conservatively dressed in plain, check, or plaid fabrics, sunny yellow walls and floral accessories soften the room.

"create a nest that's so cozy even a family of robins would feel secure."

ideal spaces for this look are under the eaves in attic areas with slanting ceilings.

FURNITURE. If your room's architecture isn't as cooperative as you'd like, enlist help from the furniture you choose. A bigger area won't look vacant and unwelcoming if you furnish it with large-scale seating pieces, a tall cabinet, or walls of bookshelf units. And in a bedroom, a canopy bed can do wonders, creating an environment for unwinding, cozying up, and recharging your spirit.

Warning: This enveloping look is not for claustrophobics! If you'd rather take the stairs than ride in a small elevator, you may want to skip to the next chapter.

If you're still with me—and since we just talked about furniture—let's take a look at the best bets in style choices for your cocoon. Generally speaking, informal, traditional furniture styles are most nurturing if you want your home to be an emotional security blanket. They're relaxed, friendly, and livable. They also give a room an ambience that may reflect roots, our childhood homes, or places and times when we felt particularly loved. Maybe the home you grew up in wasn't as informal as mine, but I could never be relaxed and comfortable in a rigidly proper room environment, no matter

COZY UP the outdoors with indoor-style comfort. The secluded feeling of this three-season porch, *opposite,* is created by the tall cabinet and potted plant, which serve as open-air "walls." The porch, *right,* relies on the surrounding foliage for its feeling of seclusion. For both porches, wicker furniture is warm and inviting.

PIONEER SPIRIT IS ALIVE AND WELL—and living with style! Not all of us can start with a chinked log cabin and stone fireplace, but we can create this same magnetic ambience anywhere we have a fireplace or stove. Start by pulling chairs in close around the fire. For cushions and fabric coverings, choose crunchy textures or patterns in traditional or ethnic designs. Handcrafted wood furniture sets a rugged tone, *above*, but the room *opposite* shows how comfortably wicker fits in too. Top the area off with warming accents in copper or brass. Then grab a book, a cup of hot cider, and settle in!

how beautiful it was. And yet that kind of studied propriety gives some people the sense of definition and security that I get from a more informally decorated room. Either personality— casual or more buttoned-up—usually leans toward traditional design rather than contemporary to help create an anchored, protective feeling in a room.

And in a warm nest that feeds your soul, furniture also has to feed your desire for physical comfort. That means seating pieces that are roomy and soft. Rockers, chaises, chairs with ottomans, down cushions, throw pillows, afghans, or lap robes cater to your comfort. Side tables and coffee tables should be big enough to hold what you want and close enough to let you reach what's on them.

How you arrange your furniture can contribute more than you might imagine to the intimate look of a room. By tightening up a furniture grouping and placing pieces closer together, you get the emotional effect of sitting in a chair and being hugged. (And all of us can use a hug once in awhile.)

COLOR is another design tool that can make a room inviting to a self-confessed "snuggler." If you're trying to visually shrink the size of your room, then dark, rich colors will do the same effective tightening job as a five-course dinner does for your waistband. In either case, nothing

actually shrinks; it just feels as though it has.

Dark colors not your taste? Then start with colors on the warm side of the color wheel (yellow, orange, red); mix them any way you like and lighten them as much as matches your mood. And although we don't think of them as part of the color family, wood and stone add color, texture, and warmth to a room.

PATTERN and color go hand-in-hand in creating an inviting, enveloping look that evokes security. The easiest, most successful pairing of patterns is stripes or checks with florals. There should be a color connecting point between patterns, but after that, the secret is to experiment until the combination pleases you. Remember, this room—like your cat when she curls up on your lap—is meant to please you and make you feel loved.

ACCESSORIES give a room the same finishing touch a cherry gives a hot fudge sundae. And while I've always found buying those personal touches just as addictive as ice cream, at least I don't have to feel guilty about any calories.

It's through a room's accessories that you express yourself and at the same time add emotion-enhancing character. The best touches for this kind of cocoon include those that create a sense of heritage and rootedness—family photos, memorabilia, books, quilts, and collectibles. These can be handed down from

YOU'LL FEEL EMBRACED when you pull furniture into a tight arrangement, *opposite*. The tray table that cozies up to the love seat and a side table almost as tall as the love seat's back help create the warm, friendly, room-hugging look. COMFORT AND WARMTH are givens in this bedroom, *above*. A petite floral design on the wallpaper and bed linens makes the space cozy and nestlike. If you don't have a real fireplace in your bedroom, consider installing a vintage mantel (or even an electric fireplace with mantel) to achieve a similar effect.

your own family or they can be things that belonged to someone else's family until you found them in antique shops or flea markets. (This decorating style is a scavenger's dream!)

LIGHTING should be soft. Use lamps rather than ceiling fixtures and place them so they bathe an area in gentle light while still providing adequate illumination for reading or activities. Three-way lamps let you control the level of light, and warm-light (incandescent) bulbs provide a welcoming glow.

How you treat the natural light in a room is up to you. You can give windows a decorative treatment or leave them basically bare and beautiful. And in many cases minimal window treatments might be best—particularly if you're like me and want to be able to see nature outside your window. When you're searching for security in an insecure world, it's comforting to look out and know that while seasons change, the beauty of nature remains constant.

OF LIGHT. "

BOOKS are friends in any sense, and here they add personality and warmth as they fill the walls—and the room—with color and pattern. The visual effect is to bring the walls in while forming a background for the red-patterned upholstered pieces, which promise all the creature comforts any reader could want.

SIMPLICITY

security
whimsy
happiness
romance
serenity
comfort
escapes
enrichment
celebration

SIMPLICITY

When my kitchen cupboards are a mess, when I can no longer see the top of my desk, when I can't find the scissors or the book I knew I put on the bookshelf, it's time to do something drastic. It's time to clean up and clean out. EASIER SAID THAN DONE!

I happen to come from a long line of pack rats and savers, so I blame genetics for my propensity to "gather." From the time I was old enough to start dragging home other kids' castoffs, my Norwegian grandmother used to say, *"Han som er spar han noget har,"* which translated means (roughly) "He who saves always has something."

The only problem is that those of us who "save" can also end up with overstuffed houses and high levels of stress and frustration—unless hide-and-seek is our favorite game.

Even I, who enjoy acquiring, have to admit that sometimes I want to EDIT MY POSSESSIONS. For others the edited look is as necessary to the way they want to live as water or air. Theirs is a no-frills, no-visual-distractions look that creates a calming, hassle-free environment while showcasing a FEW WELL-CHOSEN PIECES. Lovers of this look and lifestyle, you're definitely not alone.

A few years ago a national survey questioned American families about what they wanted most. (FYI: Wealth and prestige didn't even appear on the list.) The handsdown No. 1 item on the wish list? To SIMPLIFY THEIR LIVES—to uncomplicate them—to free up time spent with details and maintenance. SIMPLICITY!

Simplicity is good for the stressed. (And who isn't these days?) Simplicity is EASY TO LIVE WITH and easy to look at. And it may not be too far off base to say simplicity is GOOD FOR THE SOUL.

PAGE 53: A FISH OUT OF WATER becomes a room's focal point when it swims lazily over the sink in this otherwise white-on-white kitchen. The simplicity comes from limited colors, a sense of symmetry, and enough space for visual elements to float. Similar principles are at work in the dining room, *opposite,* with its ethereal white background, sleek-lined chrome table, and light-color wood. Accessories are simple and few—a rack of clear flower vials on the table, a primarily white African-design throw over the chair back, and a few understated pieces on the wooden chest. And then POW! Emerging from the white surroundings is the huge red contemporary painting—one knockout eye-catcher that sets off and emphasizes the room's simplicity.

THE GOAL a room

SIMPLICITY in design is a process of slimming down, lightening up, and tossing everything that's unnecessary or has no emotional importance to you. In other words, the space-fillers—which, incidentally, fill more than space. They also create visual clutter, eliminating the open areas that let your eye and your mind relax and appreciate the things you've elected to keep.

One of the beauties of simplification is that you can accomplish the process within the framework of your favorite design style. If you say "simple, clean, uncluttered," most people will immediately think "contemporary." But contemporary style isn't the only version of simplicity available to you. In this chapter you'll see simplified traditional, country—even Victorian. It's just a matter of following a few basic decorating premises that are dictated more by your head than your heart. Remember, what you strive to create is a room that's uncomplicated—visually and physically—one that frees you from looking at (and caring for) a lot of "stuff."

SPACE is a key factor in creating the simple look, but it's not necessarily the size of the space.

creating SIMPLICITY in a contemporary room, *opposite,* is straightforward—a neutral scheme in solid blocks of color with just enough taupe tossed in for leavening. Crisp-lined furniture floats in an island grouping, and old shutters stand in as wall-warming art. Traditional design meets simplicity through unifying color, *above.* Even the coffee table and clock, with their delicate curves, are on parade in their white dress uniforms. Clearing surfaces of unnecessary items also calms the space.

How you use (or don't use) the space is what's important. And space is the secret ingredient in the living room and dining room shown here.

All it takes is one look at these rooms to discover country style presented in a whole new way—crisp, clean, and almost graphic in the manner in which undecorated spaces are handled. The essence of this look comes from a few large-scale, focal-point primitive pieces emerging from a background of pure white space instead of being surrounded by smaller, less important furniture and accessories.

If your taste for simplicity calls for kicking up the "elements" level just a bit, you're probably a candidate for the look on page 60. The living room is painted gallery white and features large, scantily veiled windows and one large painting over the mantel-less fireplace, giving the area a simple, breath-of-fresh-air look. Still, it's comfortable and appealing through the subtle use of color, pattern, and accessories. Subtlety is a big part of simplicity.

COLOR. The more inconspicuous a room's background is, the less it will compete with your furniture and accessory choices. That doesn't mean you need to shy away from using color. Pick a color, even a strong one if you like, but put it to work unifying and simplifying the walls of your room. Avoid using high-contrast color accents. They'll give the area a shot of visual stimulation you don't need when you're trying to create an easygoing, laid-back atmosphere. For the same reason, you're wise to limit the

COUNTRY SIMPLICITY? These two rooms prove country can be simple and elegant without giving up any of its character or heritage. A heart-of-country color scheme of red, white, and blue carries through the decor, *opposite* and *above*. In both rooms, the furnishings are sparse, letting each well-chosen country primitive piece stand out against a backdrop of shimmering white. Accessories are few, carefully selected, and placed with the eye of an artist. And the symmetry of the dining room furniture arrangement, *above*, also adds to the order of the room. Less of everything, that's the key to country simplicity—a far cry from yesterday's heavily accessorized country style.

WHITE WORKS WONDERS in this simple, subtle, and very sophisticated home, *above* and *opposite*. In the color scheme of things, white comes in more varieties than you'd think—from cool grayed whites to warm whites approaching beige. For visual interest, plan to use several shades in combination. Accessories in simplified decorating schemes don't overpower. In both these rooms quantity is limited and color is subdued. And in the kitchen, *opposite*, the open shelves become a graphic work of art through the repetition of items on each shelf—all in some shade of white (or a near neighbor). While there are actually a lot of utilitarian items stored within easy reach, the area becomes quietly decorative with a tidiness that is part of simplifying your decorating scheme—and your life.

number of colors you introduce in your room. Think of each color as a cup of high-octane coffee. How many can you drink in one sitting without getting wired? And if you're working to uncomplicate your decorating scheme, what it needs least of all is a case of the jitters.

Of course, a white-on-white color scheme is the epitome of simplicity. A single light color—either white or pastel—makes the room look bigger, more open, and less confining. And combining white with one other carefully chosen color, or with wood, still injects enough interest to intrigue the eye without turning your quiet room into the at-home equivalent of a video arcade.

Another plan for keeping a room's background subdued is the use of neutral colors—from sand to chocolate, slate, and ebony—and natural materials that are smooth, not heavily textured.

PATTERN is a possibility, but only when used deftly. Most simplified interiors are patternless or limit fabric interest to texture rather than risk using a design that could busy-up the look of a room. If you do opt for a pattern in fabric, a geometric is easier to fit into your room than a floral. In either case, make sure colors in the pattern are closely related and low in contrast.

FURNITURE gives your room its style direction. For a simplified decorating look, you're going to have to give up the curlicues. I bet if simplicity appeals to you, you're not really into Louis XV furniture anyway. Your best option is to pick furniture pieces with style (whichever suits your taste) but with clean lines. Think about the time you'll have to spend dusting and you'll automatically avoid unsuitable choices.

If you have—or find and love—some really spectacular piece of furniture, go for it. But give it its own staging area where it can make a statement and not compete with the rest of the furniture in your room. Consider it an accessory.

Furniture that's fairly large in scale works well in a simplified room. The reason: If you didn't have one large sofa or chair, you might be inclined to use several smaller pieces. And the more individual items you add to a room, the less simple the room's character becomes.

ARRANGEMENT. The way you arrange your furniture also contributes to the look of a room. A seating group that floats in the room is more attractive than one that's shoved up against the walls. There's breathing room in this kind of arrangement that's all part of the freed-up feeling you're striving for. If you grew up with furniture clinging to the walls like morning glories on a trellis, break out! Play with arrangements. Try some island groupings. You will be surprised how liberated your room looks when you can glimpse baseboard here and there.

WHITE ON WHITE might sound like a cold and boring way to decorate a room, but not so! The interest created by two different style chairs, one understated but impressive centerpiece on the table, and the play of light through the multipaned windows makes the room anything but static. Fine-line touches of black provide the contrasting note that sparks the scheme.

"SIMPLIFY FOR IMPACT."

LIGHT. While light may not seem like something you need to consider in simplifying the overall look of a room, don't underestimate what it can do for visual space. If you're blessed with supersized windows, take advantage of them and let sunlight stream in. Not only does bright light make your room look larger, its optical effect is to emphasize the importance of a few larger pieces of furniture—to put them in the spotlight and give them breathing room. And the play of light and shadows falling on walls and floors adds simple beauty and interior interest without demanding more furnishings or accessories.

If you need light control or privacy, think about blinds or shades, a slim, noncluttering solution to the problem. Choices in blinds include either horizontal or vertical slats in a variety of widths, materials, and colors. If you prefer a less architectural look, consider Roman shades; they fold up into neat, flat panels as you raise them, softening the look of the windows without being fussy.

By all means, do the bare minimum for window coverings. Save overly decorative, detailed window treatments for another time (and the pendulum does swing) when simplicity and easy maintenance may not be high on your agenda.

Artificial lighting should be considered the same way natural lighting is. Work toward a lighting scheme that provides soft, diffused,

SIMPLIFY WITH COLOR. Neutrals—primarily beige and gray—offer the same soft, simple background, *opposite*, as white. They merely alter the room's color temperature slightly. Grayed neutrals will cool a room while tones of beige will warm it. A SINGLE COLOR, no matter how strong, can still create a backdrop for simplicity, *above*. In this living room, red adds color interest without busy distractions. Your best bet: Keep your palette scaled back to one color. Adding others will only foster the visual busy-ness you're trying to avoid.

well-balanced light in your room. Your best choices here are lamps and fixtures that are simple, clean-lined, and unobtrusive.

ACCESSORIES can make or break your room's transition to simplification. Let's take this from the top: The 20th-century modernist architect Mies van der Rohe had it right when he said, "Less is more!"

When it comes to creating design simplicity, wall space is your best asset. Don't clobber it! Choose accessories with care and don't get carried away. One large accent piece will do more for your emotional and visual freedom than a whole roomful of small-scale doodads, no matter how precious each one is individually. The more accessories you add, the more complicated your environment becomes.

I know this sounds hard and cruel to those of us who are attached to "things," but for anyone whose psyche is nurtured by open space, clean lines, and visual tranquillity—for anyone who is striving to simplify life—it's the only way to go.

FURNITURE ARRANGEMENT can make or break the simplicity of your room. Pulling furniture away from the walls, *below*, lets it float, giving the area a clean, light, uncomplicated look. In a dining spot, *opposite*, the table and chairs are by necessity pulled away from the wall, but the absence of an area rug under the table also contributes to the look of uncluttered simplicity. Hanging a single large painting instead of a grouping of smaller pieces enhances simplicity with a strong, straightforward focal point.

SECURITY
SIMPLICITY
WHIMSY
HAPPINESS
ROMANCE
SERENITY
COMFORT
ESCAPES
ENRICHMENT
CELEBRATION

WHIMSY

Sometimes, when I'm bogged down by work or finances or home maintenance challenges, I (like you, I'm sure) wonder what happened to the easygoing, Free-spirited person I used to be. And I ask myself, how do I get her back?

The answer comes when I sit down and think of things that make me feel truly carefree and lighthearted—silly things, maybe, but spirit-brighteners, nonetheless.

My list is long and touches most of my senses. And while these may not be anyone else's "uppers," some of mine are: watermelon,

Viennese waltzes, kaleidoscopes, kites, and puppies playing. But carousels top the list.

Ever since I was a kid I've been mesmerized and happy watching the swan benches glide by and the gaudy painted horses prance up and down to tinny calliope music. Who can take things seriously when you're watching (or riding) a merry-go-round? And what's its magic? It's the COLOR AND FANTASY—it takes you back to those days of childhood when things didn't have to be so serious.

Since there will always be a bit of "kid" in me, I truly believe it's possible (and even easy) to TOUCH YOUR LIFE and your home with bits of whimsy. In this chapter you'll see some gentle rib-ticklers that will make you realize it's perfectly all right TO HAVE A LITTLE FUN WITH YOUR DECORATING and to inject a little humor into your home.

Life is too short to be buttoned-up serious 24/7. Just kick up your decorating heels ever so slightly and see how much fun you can have. My advice is: Go ahead, let your hair down, and for an instant, it might just feel like your little girl pigtails are flying out behind you as you charge around the carousel on a brightly painted horse.

PAGE 71: AN ANTIQUE ADVERTISING SIGN hangs from a wall-mounted bracket, and the village of primitive birdhouses becomes the perfect cabinet-top aviary/accessory. A PARADE OF LONG-STEMMED POSIES brings quirky personality to a bathroom shelf, *opposite*. The whimsy results from contrast: Identical, clean-lined glass vases sporting gangly stems and bobble-head blossoms have a modern look while the botanical print, beaded board paneling, and sink fixtures suggest vintage, cottage-style charm. If the flowers were roses and the containers milk-glass pitchers, the effect would be entirely different —romantic rather than humorous.

a room that makes you smile, the kit

Some things in life you have to take seriously. Home decorating isn't one of them! As a matter of fact, creating a one-of-a-kind, eye-catching room can be as much fun as a leprechaun's romp through a field of shamrocks. The fun—and the magic—comes from whimsy.

The only problem is that whimsy is ephemeral and hard to define. Maybe the best way to define it is to think of whimsy the same way you would a limerick—it starts out with a believable premise and ends with a quirky twist. It would be like deciding to repaint your bedroom, then capping it off with clouds painted on the ceiling. Whimsy is lighthearted, ebullient, slightly offbeat, and unexpected. It's anything but run-of-the-mill.

The important thing to remember about whimsy is that it touches the surface but not the substance of your room. Your flip little accents should be just that—accents. And they should be easily replaced or removed when they've played out their season. Anything as attention-getting as the whimsical elements of a room will, in time, lose their fresh, entertaining appeal and become as tired (and tiring) as a joke the third or fourth time you've heard it.

MAD FOR MATISSE! He's the early 20th-century artist whose paper collages and paintings inspired this lighthearted bedroom, *opposite* and *left*. The framed poster in the corner, the blue nude tiles on the window seat, and contemporary fabrics bearing his signature graphic shapes and bold colors express a spirit of gaiety that has more staying power than most sources of whimsy. Another easy-to-live-with source of decorating playfulness: boldly colored quilts folded to show off their graphic patterns on open shelves.

COLOR can provide a short, snappy jolt for a room that needs to be liberated from hidebound rules or anyone else's expectations. For fast, relatively inexpensive whops of color, use paint. Pick it bright and put it in places you'd least expect to find it—on a door, inside a cabinet, or on the floor.

The most common overall coloration for this kind of engaging room is light, bright, and happy. No matter what kind of insouciant accessories you use, you'll never achieve the I-don't-give-a-hoot look in a room that's painted a dark, somber color.

FABRIC is another way to give your room a mild shock (a tingle, really) of bold color. It can be used as effectively as paint, but it's even more transient. Now you see it, now you don't. To tease a room's sense of humor with fabric, use eye-opening patterns (gargantuan geometrics are great for a whimsically contemporary room) to cover pillows and beds, drape over curtain rods, or frame as wall art.

PATTERN in a whimsy-filled room is a question of "to be or not to be." You can add to your room's whimsical looks with carefree prints—such as a signature pattern covering a chair. In other cases a more neutral, low-key pattern approach is the perfect foil for

ONE QUILT can turn a sofa into a showpiece, *opposite,* but using lots of quilts in a room can give the whole area the RAZZLE-DAZZLE of a piece of millefiori glass, *above.* If you're blessed with quilts, don't hide them, just snitch some decorating tips from this whimsical cottage. But take precautions too. For instance, don't expose a quilt to direct sunlight or its color will fade and the fabric weaken. If you hang a quilt on the wall, carefully handstitch a fabric rod pocket to the quilt back and slip it onto a sturdy dowel. As any quilt person knows, it's a sacrilege to nail a quilt to the wall.

imaginative accents that deliver their own kind of chuck under the chin to bring on smiles.

THE ELEMENT OF SURPRISE needs to be considered in creating whimsy because it's not always just a matter of what you include in your room, but where you put it. Luckily, the only limit to your success is your imagination, and anything short of outrageous works to your advantage. For example, try a floor rug on a wall, a hammock inside the house, or a flock of flamingos in your backyard—even though you live thousands of miles from a tropical beach.

ACCESSORIES are the smile-makers in your decorating scheme. Sometimes all it takes is one spectacular, tongue-in-cheek accessory such as the flamboyantly faux wooden hollyhocks blooming in a summertime fireplace (page 80). Or go for something as far out as the neon parrot perched in a kitchen filled with eye-popping dishware, *right,* and you've created a look to tickle anyone's funny bone.

Whimsy is inventive. It's doing your own thing in the most blatant ways possible. And creating it is nothing you hire a designer to do.

A TONGUE-IN-CHEEK touch makes a room more fun. In the kitchen, *right,* it's a neon Polly wanting a cracker. Shop antiques stores for vintage neon signs or design your own and have it made by a commercial firm (check the *Yellow Pages* under Neon). The SMILE-INDUCING accent in the kitchen, *opposite,* is cutlery that's missed the drawer and ended up on the cabinet doors. Stenciling the motifs on white painted doors is an easy do-it-yourself project.

It's too personal. It relies too heavily on your sense of humor—your taste.

To get started, think as far out of the box as you can. How about lining a kitchen windowsill with plants in food cans that still have their labels? Or create a backsplash above your kitchen counter with a gallery of your child's (or grandchild's) art in plastic photo frames.

While there's no way to solidly pin down "whimsy" in decorating and there's no specific recipe for creating it, it's safe to say it's really 50 percent creativity and 50 percent courage. It's original and ingenious. It can be anything you want it to be and it should be decorating simply for the fun of it. And when you pull it off, a whimsical room is as infectious as a gaggle of little girls with the giggles.

WOOD IS THE CHIEF INGREDIENT in these whimsies—wood, a little paint, and a whole lot of imagination. In the off-season, the fireplace *opposite* turns garden, all neatly tucked behind a white picket fence. The fanciful hollyhocks are double-layered to give them dimension and hinged to fold like a screen. The demilune table, *left,* sports an apron created from bits of cast-off siding and molding in various styles and colors. This is an easy way to dress up a garage sale table or console. Painting the tabletop and legs a solid color focuses attention on the multicolored moldings, which are simply attached with wood glue and brads.

WHIMSY WORKS

WHIMSY IS ABOUT DOING THE UNEXPECTED. Who would expect a grapevine hanging from a high wall shelf, *opposite?* Yet it's just the right touch in a family room that's gearing up for pumpkin time. Or how about the swinging furniture arrangement *above?* The hammock looks just as inviting and comfortable inside as it does outdoors. See what the latest tropical storm brought in—a whole flock of landlocked flamingos, looking flamboyantly exotic in an ocean of ferns, *above right.* Don't like to shake out rugs? Then paint one on the floor, *below right.* Use epoxy paint or cement paint on concrete floors, latex paint for wood surfaces.

SECURITY
SIMPLICITY
WHIMSY
HAPPINESS
ROMANCE
SERENITY
COMFORT
ESCAPES
ENRICHMENT
CELEBRATION

Happiness

When MY 3-YEAR-OLD GRANDSON comes running toward me to give me a hug–his blueberry-color eyes sparkling and his chubby little arms widespread–I'm in heaven! That's pure joy! And when he plants a sloppy little-boy kiss on my face, it's like a benediction. In that moment life is rainbows, bright balloons, circus music, and all the things that make me happiest.

For me happiness ALWAYS HAS COME FROM SIMPLE THINGS. I'd rather be OUT IN MY GARDEN with the early morning birds, watching the sun come up, than be in Paris shopping the famous fashion

houses on the Rue St. Germaine. Watching 4TH OF JULY FIreworks thrills me more than attending the Academy Awards ceremony ever would. And a HANDFUL OF DAISIES from little Noah makes me happier than a headlight-size diamond from a millionaire.

Those moments of happiness, no matter when or where they happen, fill my world with COLOr anD BEAUTY and make me want to hold on to them forever—even though I know that's impossible.

But I've been in the design business long enough to know there are visual stimuli that can go a long way toward holding on to happiness—or at least helping you feel upbeat. You might be surprised at the DIFFerence In your mooD if you're surrounded by one color rather than another. Or at the way you feel in different kinds of light. Some patterns are day-brighteners too. It's a matter of knowing which decorating tools to use and how to use them.

Cheating? I don't think so. This kind of decorating isn't creating false happiness; it's creating a room environment that supports anD nurtures the brighter side of life. It may not be a kiss from someone you love, but a room that sparkles with light and color naturally lifts your spirits and makes you feel good.

PAGE 87: a BIG DOSE OF SUNSHINE—real or simulated—can't help but bring on the smiles. The natural sunlight in this room is augmented (or replaced on rainy days) by sunshine yellow fabric at the windows and on the wicker daybed and chair. Light and sunny, cozy and bright—good ingredients for creating happiness. LIVELY, COLOrFUL stripes and florals cheer a room furnished with white wicker, *opposite*. For even more upbeat touches, lattice layers over the lower section of the windows and a collection of old wicker flower baskets lines the shelf. (A plastic cup that fits into the basket serves as a watertight liner for fresh flowers.)

THE GOAL a room as cheering

Most of us feel better when the sun is shining than we do on dark, rainy days (unless we've got closets to clean or a good book half-read). That same kind of mood manipulation takes place inside a home too. People generally feel cheerier, happier, and more energized in rooms washed with sun-stroked colors than they do enveloped by the quiet, cool colors used to create relaxed, tranquil settings.

As a rule, COLORS that promote a feeling of happiness most often come from the warm side of the color wheel (yellow, orange, red). They can be bold and saturated or softened with white to create a more lighthearted look. And which way you go depends entirely on your threshold for color intensity. Some people like a conservative approach to making a color statement while others feel best when they're hit with a real wallop of color. (Tip: If your room is sunny and bright, you can cut back on the strength of the color you use on walls. The sunlight will intensify it naturally—with no help

WARM COLORS, plus a sun-dazzled floral print teamed with relaxed awning stripes, will go a long way toward creating a happy, bubbly interior. The sherbet-hued plaid rug inspires this room's palette of pastel colors. Combining the stripe and the floral on one sofa creates a mix-and-match cottage-style look; slipcovering a second sofa in solid white gives the eye a rest from all the pattern. Crisp white on the woodwork, fireplace, and wicker coffee table perks up the ambience too.

as SUNSHINE, a CHILD'S LaUGHTer, or YOUR FavORITe DesseRT. "

from your friendly neighborhood paint dealer.)

You can use just one happy color or combine it with others. Pick-me-up colors can be applied to walls, furniture, or accents, or to all three. Color can dominate a room, or you can keep your room a neutral white and pepper it with bright accent hues. The decision is personal and based on whatever balance of color makes you feel best.

If you do plan to mix colors in a room, it's a good idea to have one dominant color with other hues taking subordinate roles. That's the safest way to play this game, but that's not the only way. You'll see rooms in this chapter where colors (and really strong colors at that) have been splashed around an area in fairly equal quantities in fabric and in paint, and the effect is nothing short of exhilarating. However, if this is the effect you want and you're a newcomer to blending colors, it may be wise to consult a design professional for advice.

PATTERN. Be sure to include pattern when you want to give your room a lively, up-tempo look. For even more spark, choose more than one pattern and combine them. Just keep all the patterns within your color scheme and you'll be safe.

FIRE ENGINE RED sizzles floor to ceiling in a relatively small room, *above*. Red sparks more energy than a docile color would, and when it's countered by pristine white in woodwork and upholstery, it's a four-alarm success. FURNITURE AND ACCESSORIES, rather than the walls, supply the color personality in this living room, *opposite*. The citrusy color scheme and neutral background start you on the road to happiness, but the real keys are the accessories. Objects that spark interest, inspire exploration, and recall fun places or great vacations (surely there's a story behind the old oar leaning on the fireplace wall) raise the room's happiness quotient by reminding you of good times and good feelings. Arrange them sparingly for a clean, architectural effect or cluster them if you prefer the collector's-closet look.

CERTAIN COLOR SCHEMES were born to be crowd pleasers. The mix of blue and yellow is one. Some say it has its roots in country French interiors, others say the color scheme speaks with a Swedish accent. Either way, it's a surefire winner when you want a room that promotes happiness. While the colors don't vary in this cottage, there's a rich mix of patterns. In the living room, *above*, a quilt-design area rug, floral print fabric, even an eye-catching tile treatment on the fireplace carry out the color scheme. In the bedroom, *opposite*, the same scheme plays out but yellow dominates, with a pattern mix of yellow stripes and a blue and yellow quilt.

When you're shopping for patterns, it helps to understand their characteristics. Florals, for example, have a natural, carefree look about them and combine well with checks, stripes, or geometrics. In the case of both florals and straight-line patterns, go for larger scale designs to create an informal and fun room. Avoid the crisp tidiness of small-scale designs. If you're not careful, they can generate an uptight, businesslike look that's guaranteed to squelch your room's happy feeling faster than a swarm of wasps at a family picnic.

THINGS that make you happy should be included in your joy-filled room. Books, your piano, favorite art—they all add their own invitation to happiness. This room also is a great place to display photos of special people and times, or treasures you associate with family and fun. If you paint, do needlework, or anything creative, use this room to show off your accomplishments. It will make you feel wonderful to see what you've done.

NATURAL LIGHT streaming through the windows is as good as Tinkerbell's wand for touching the room with a sparkling glow. And if your room is situated so the windows scoop up southern light, so much the better. The more windows a room has, the easier it is for you to boost its happiness quotient. But what you do

(or don't do) by way of window treatments is as important as the number, size, or location of the windows themselves. To take the best advantage of the windows and the light, shy away from any covering at all. Of course, if privacy or light control is a consideration, you'll have to do something at the windows, but go easy and keep it minimal.

If you can get by with it, a treatment of light gauze or semisheer fabric will give you a hint of covering but still let in nearly as much light as no covering at all. Other almost-nothing window treatments are translucent fabric shades that offer protection while still providing a soft glow of light. They also have the advantage of pulling up to become nearly invisible when you want to let the light pour in.

Shutters are another good choice. They can be opened, closed, or adjusted for just the right light without obliterating the view.

Consider artificial lighting when planning your feel-good room. If using fluorescent fixtures, definitely opt for warm bulbs, not cool

sun-up color and light...just perfect.

WALKING INTO THIS ROOM is like taking a big breath of fresh air. Some of the light, airy feeling comes from a slimmed-down furniture arrangement; some from spacious windows trimmed with simple tieback panels. The real joy, however, comes from the focal-point wall of shelves loaded with books. In a low-key color scheme like this, nothing competes with personal spirit-lifters, so keep the background warm and neutral, then add your favorite treasures.

ones. Place lamps around a room to create a uniform overall light so that even on a dull day (or in the evening) you can bask in simulated sunshine. And for a still warmer glow, choose pink lightbulbs.

If you genuinely suffer without sunshine, SAD (Seasonal Affective Disorder) bulbs, available at lighting stores, fight the sunless blahs quite effectively.

Now that you have the recipe for a spirit-lifting decorating scheme, maybe it's time to listen again to the advice of Judy Garland (not best known as a counselor, but she had a good idea here). In the movie *Summer Stock*, Ms. Garland—wearing a jaunty hat, man's tuxedo jacket, and black tights—belted out "Forget your troubles, come on, get happy!" Who can argue with that?

A ROOM THAT SPARKLES with personal touches is guaranteed to create little bursts of happiness. In this pale-blue and white kitchen, *below*, the do-it-yourself painted and stenciled cabinets are a labor of love that pays big dividends in the satisfaction that comes from personal creative expression. THE LOVE (and the happiness) in this kitchen, *opposite*, comes from collecting, displaying, and using antique kitchen utensils and accessories. The view beyond the sink lifts the spirits too.

THE RIGHT LIGHT plays a big part in how carefree and happy you feel in a room. And sometimes you need to employ some easy decorating techniques to take full advantage of a room's wattage. First, furniture soaks up light, so keep your furniture arrangement slimmed down, *opposite*. Because curlicues are light-catchers, too, simple-lined tables and chairs work best, *above left*. Next, resist covering your windows—that lets you scoop as much light into the room as you can. Finally, light colors reflect light and dark colors absorb it. So keep your color schemes upbeat and sunny, *below left*.

PATTERN AND COLOR combine to create this lively room, *above right*. Where do you start? This room was inspired by the insects that fly and crawl across the fabric of the coverlet and edge the checked dust ruffles on the twin beds. Instead of a valance, a colorful bee, fashioned from fabric, buzzes at the top of the window. And what fun are bees without blossoms? A fanciful bouquet of stylized flowers decorates the wall between the beds. The yellow, orange, and red color scheme continues in the wall painting, as well as accenting the beds' footboards. Even the room's offbeat color highlights—the shades of blue in the bed throws and pillows—combine with enough orange to blend them into this fun and fanciful bug cage of a bedroom.

SECURITY
SIMPLICITY
WHIMSY
HAPPINESS
romance
SERENITY
COMFORT
escapes
enrichment
celebration

romance

I may have to disqualify myself from writing this chapter. It isn't that I'm not a romantic. Deep down inside, I am. I love flowers, the glow of a fireplace, starlit nights, champagne, and chick flicks with disgustingly sappy-happy endings. Happy endings make me cry. So do sad endings. As a matter of fact, nearly everything that touches a **HUMAN EMOTION** makes me cry. It's ridiculous, but the telephone company commercials that showed family members sharing their joy across miles of technology were always a six-tissue moment for me. That's the "INSIDE" me—the romantic me.

How the world sees me, however, may be quite different. If I'm realistic, I expect people who don't know me well would view me as anything but romantic—too practical, too professional—the do-it-yourself homeowner and gardener, editor, writer, businesswoman. I'm too "tomboy" in my figure, too tailored in my dress.

However, if I turn myself inside out and let the closet romantic loose, I can clearly understand all the home decorating qualities that nurture the SOFTER, MORE DELICATE side of human nature. I might not decorate my own home in this particular style, but I can appreciate it. And if you're the type who wants to FEEL LIKE A PRINCESS in her very own castle, surrounded by beautiful design "jewels" set in a shimmering, soft setting, I can wave a magic decorating wand and help you get there. It's just a matter of understanding the elements that blend best to create a romantic look—the delicate shades of color, the SUBTLE WASH of patterns, the gently lined furniture, and most of all, the stage-setting accessories. Ready to go? Just close your eyes, click your red-sequined shoes together, and we're off to a romantic interior.

PAGE 105: AH, SWEET ROMANCE. Flowers, especially roses, are key to romantic style. If this is your look, you're likely to start outdoors with a lush, gently untamed cottage garden that welcomes visitors to your door. Indoors you'll opt for FLORAL MOTIFS, soft colors, and furnishings with graceful curves like the Italian table *opposite*. Its finish of gold leaf and porcelain ivory shows off delicate accessories, including a silver urn filled with the signature of romantic style—wide open, sinfully seductive roses. And that's another point: Whether you grow your own flowers or buy a bouquet at the grocery store, TREAT YOURSELF to fresh blossoms to bring romance to your rooms.

The romantic look is easy, as long as you love roses—blowsy, full-blown, sun-ripened roses. It certainly isn't that roses are the only design motif allowed. It is, more than anything else, the *character* of roses—sensuous, opulent, lush, and yes, romantic—that also characterizes a romantic room.

COLOR is most romantic if it's soft, pastel, and tinged with a blush of warmth. Cool colors, however, can work almost as well if they show up in their very lightest tints.

Today most rooms that evoke romance are light and delicate in their overall essence, showcasing a quiet, gentle style. Think of your romantic room as poetry by Elizabeth Barrett Browning—not the explicit prose of today's romance writers. In this style it's perfectly appropriate for walls to wear some discreet

WHILE FLOWERS are important in a romantic look, they don't have to cover every surface to act as Cupid's helpers. Creamy walls and woodwork are a whisper-quiet background for a mix of patterns that, while different from each other, share the same muted coloration. Botanical prints and a floral still life are obvious choices for the mantel, where they echo the romance of upholstery and accessories.

romance 109

jewelry—crown molding or paneled insets that are painted a secondary soft color. And if you use wallcoverings, they should be limited to petite floral prints, very quiet stripes, or paper that simulates a watercolor-washed painted finish. You don't want your walls to be the strong focus in a romantic room. They should be demure backgrounds for all the visual allure that comes from the furniture, window treatments, and accessories.

PATTERN in fabric is primarily floral, although pastel stripes or traditional toile de Jouy (the 18th century pastoral prints) are other favorite motifs.

SOFT SAGE GREEN and white tinged with a blush of pink set up the color scheme for romance, *above*. The mantel's sensuous curves repeat along the bottom edges of the sofa slipcovers to give this room grace and femininity. COZY describes the corner *opposite*, with its mixed patterns in soft pastel colors and tabletop gallery of family photos. The floral abundance softens the rugged exposed brick and plank walls to evoke comfy cottage style.

antiques make the mix unique.

antique wicker conjures sentimental, nostalgic images even in today's homes. And the beauty of wicker, antique or not, is that it's light in scale and open in appearance, so it brings a sense of expansiveness and airiness that visually weighty wood or upholstered pieces would not. Wicker also lends a tinge of Victoriana to a room. In this room the deep, fringed valances and gilt-framed wall pieces support the turn-of-the-20th-century look, as does the tabletop dressed in its best china and bouquets of fresh flowers.

CONTRASTING STYLES play off each other to give this room its dressed-up cottage character. The buttoned-up formality of the camelback sofa, with its carved wood and neat stripes, is relaxed by the white plank wall and wicker side table. And if there's any stuffiness left about the classic sofa, it's warmed and offset by the bank of pillows in their typically romantic fabrics—floral designs, muted colors, and the soft look of age. You can use reproduction vintage fabrics, but it's more fun to shop antiques stores.

And since we can't talk romantic pattern without trumpeting roses, let's clarify that in this case, Gertrude Stein was *not* right when she said "a rose is a rose is a rose." There are no tight little rosebuds or half-open hybrids here. The romantic look calls for roses that are fully open and look like they lost their innocence in the sunshine of Provence.

FABRIC plays a big role in touching your room's heartstrings. Here's the place to use lace, embroidery, crochet, even touches of brocade. And use fabrics lavishly. If one table covering is nice, two are a knockout when it comes to creating romance. Layer bed coverings too, starting with a dust ruffle, adding a quilt or coverlet, then topping it all off with a flock of decorative pillows. Soft is the operative word for a romantic decorating scheme—soft colors, soft surfaces—and nothing creates "soft" like fabrics.

FURNITURE for a romantic room should continue the softening process. Lines should be fluid, upholstery squishy-comfortable, and each piece should give you license to be a little frivolous, whether it's a glimpse of carved wood on an upholstered piece or a simulated gold-leaf finish on a cabinet.

Favorite furniture finishes for this look include painted or stenciled, plus extremes that range from slightly distressed woods to highly polished mahogany or cherry. Wicker,

a WHIPPED-cream color, blue, and white are the mainstays in the dining area, *opposite*, that smacks of Gustavian style. But the Swedes of Gustav's time never decorated so lavishly—pattern on pattern, lace over fabric, and a comfortable mix of furniture styles. aLL WHITE IS aLL rIGHT, as the dining room *above* eloquently demonstrates. There are, however, hints of bluish white and creamy white to counter the stark white that used alone would look too antiseptic. Also on display is the skilled use of scale to offset the heady look of an all-white room. The sturdy table base, for instance, does more than support the tabletop. It and the lighted corner cabinet provide some much needed ballast and add carved details to the understated room.

rattan, and wrought iron also fit nicely into a romantic atmosphere, if the pieces are delicate.

ACCESSORIES favor (you guessed it) floral patterns—floral-patterned china, botanical prints, framed floral embroidered panels, and floral area rugs. But don't panic about turning all those floral patterns loose in your room. Vary the scale of the designs and limit the range of the colors and you'll find you've created the same effect as an old-fashioned flower garden. If flower gardens don't appeal to you, cut back on the profuse use of pattern and you can still enjoy the same soft, beautiful effect, only on a smaller scale. (Maybe you'd rather plant a window box than a big, rambling flower garden anyway.)

Some important accessories for romancing a room are chandeliers, mirrors with ornate frames, silver pieces, crystal, majolica, and quilts. If you're using quilts, choose patterns that mix soft colors in an overall design. Avoid strong colors or high-contrast, focal-point patterns.

LIGHT needs to be soft and diffused if you want to visually enhance the delicate beauty of your room. This style is perfect for decorative wall sconces and chandeliers. But don't forget the dimmer switches. They're as important to a romantic room as soft music and candlelight.

There's only one more ingredient to mention if what you're cooking up is a love potion for your room—window treatments. If you've been quietly patient through all the chapters

ROMANTIC BEDROOMS can be subtle like the one, *above,* in its white dress. Dark accents—in the headboard, table, antique chair, and lampshade—serve as a satisfying counterpoint to the white fabrics, creating a serene, sophisticated look. The bedroom, *opposite,* takes the opposite approach, bridging the contrast between dark and light with pattern. The floral bedding links the dark tones of the paneled walls and mahogany bed to the crisp white of the bed skirt, pillows, and tablecloth, creating a more traditional interpretation of romance.

advocating minimal window coverings, here's your chance to express yourself with no holds barred. Romantic windows usually are dressed in high style with several layers of fabric, plus swags and jabots if you like. This also is a decorating style that lets you use fabric extravagantly with curtain panels puddling onto the floor in graceful swirls. And remember, for the most romantic effect, a window covering should be as soft and free-flowing as a summer gown in an evening breeze.

ROMANTIC STYLE doesn't have to drip roses to be successful. In the guest room *opposite*, sedate yellow and white striped walls, a Craftsman-style bed, and pastel quilts set the tone. The only de rigueur romantic elements are the accessories on the built-in shelves. ONE SWAG is good, but two are even better, *below left*; and for the perfect romantic touch, the two panels are allowed to swirl in a puddle of fabric on the floor. The painted bedside table echoes the floral theme of the fabric and adds punch to the room's color palette. EMBROIDERED LACE sheers framed by floral-print panels, *below right*, offer a less structured but equally romantic solution to dressing the windows. The table, a flea market find, reaches mattress height so it's perfect for bedside duty. The ample top provides room for books, collections, and the essential reading lamp.

INDOORS OR OUT, romance is completely at home. And many of the style's identifying characteristics work as well in either place. That means slip in some roses when you can; when you can't, hydrangeas will be just fine. Other symbols of outdoor romance are painted metal accessories with a timeworn look and furniture with that same patina—real or induced. Whites are romantic anywhere, as are botanical prints (yes, even on outside walls).

"romance knows no boundaries."

SECURITY
SIMPLICITY
WHIMSY
HAPPINESS
romance

serenity

comfort
escapes
enrichment
celebration

serenity

Growing up in the country provided me with plenty of peace and quiet. The only problem was that, to a kid, there's a fine line between "PEACE AND QUIET" and "boredom." Summers seemed endless— nothing to do, no friends to play with. The only time I saw any of my school friends was Sunday morning, and there wasn't a whole lot of revelry going on in a straitlaced Norwegian Lutheran church.

By the time I reached high school, my summers were filled with band practice, a part-time job, and shopping trips to town. Around then, something else happened. I began to realize that a little peace

and quiet wasn't so bad after all. It actually felt good to STEP OFF THE TREADMILL every so often.

It was at those times I wanted most to spend lazy hours in our backyard hammock that was hung between two giant maple trees. I loved watching the light and shadows as the monochromatic sea of green leaves swayed and shifted in a soft breeze.

I got that same REMOVED-FROM-THE-WORLD feeling of tranquillity sitting on the dock at our family cabin on a quiet little inland lake (before the days of personal watercrafts). Wonderful thoughts—or no thoughts at all—filled the minutes I spent watching puffy clouds chase each other across the sky while I hoped that any fish in the area would ignore my hook and swim on by. Fishing was just my excuse for sitting on the dock doing nothing (not a good thing in a workaholic family) but I didn't want to be bothered by fish. I rarely baited the hook.

For me serenity is profoundly connected to nature. There's a QUIETING EFFECT IN NATURAL THINGS. In all of us there's a DEEP NEED for serenity—for GETTING AWAY AND HEALING.

The good news is that it's possible to create that same kind of relaxing, RESTORATIVE SPACE in and around our own homes.

PAGE 125. QUIET AND CALM as a still lake at sunrise, this bedroom soothes in every way—physically, emotionally, and visually—with its understated furnishings and light color scheme, a soft duet of creamy white and taupe. Checked draperies, French doors, a straight-lined chair, and the iron bed share a clean geometry that produces a wonderful sense of order, inviting you to relax. DREAMERS, MEDITATORS, the secluded spot *opposite* is for you. A single Adirondack chair nestles into a corner of the garden, offering sweet scents and summer sounds. In your search for serenity, you couldn't ask for more.

You can't bottle and sell serenity, but you can create it.

COLOR is a great ally in bringing this feeling to any area of your home. Just remember, if you want the calming effect of nature, use nature's colors—the white of clouds, the soft neutrals of desert or beach sand, and the whole spectrum of blues from water and sky.

Because color and color schemes create strong emotional reactions, avoid bright, stimulating, provocative colors or high-contrast color schemes. There are plenty of places in your home to use strong colors, but your serenity room isn't one of them.

Decorating with brilliant reds or oranges would produce about as much tranquillity as inviting in a rock band for background music. Serenity spaces invite you to whisper—or not talk at all—and you'll achieve this ambience best

WHAT LUXURY TO refresh your spirit and ease your tension in a bedroom like this! If you have the space, carve out a seating area for lounging or reading. Load your bed with comforters and swathe the whole room in calming white, with only a touch of a second light color. In the best of all worlds, the pièce de résistance would be your own spa.

" THE GOAL a PLACE THAT LETS YOU FEEL AS PEACEFUL AS a KITTEN SLEEPING IN THE SUN. "

with soft colors, muted tones, and low-contrast color schemes.

White is a longtime favorite in tranquil settings, as are other light, cool colors. It's important to stay on the cool side of the color wheel (green, blue, purple) and avoid hot, strong hues. Even when you start with cool colors, plan to lighten them to pastel tints and possibly touch them with a hint of gray to subdue them even further.

Monochromatic color schemes work best in a room where you want to relax. Various shades of one color will give your room quiet visual interest without upsetting its tranquillity.

If your psyche relaxes more completely in a darker, cocoonlike setting, that's fine too. Just pick one deep, luxurious color (either cool or neutral) and use it in your room from top to

CRAWLING INTO A CLOUD describes what it's like to walk into these two rooms, *right* and *opposite*. There are no jarring colors or strong patterns to jangle your nerves, only a soft blend of feathery white and creamy off-white. Accessories, too, are keyed to the hushed quiet of the room's decor. The wicker chair, *right,* sports a light blue pillow and has a matching side table, but that's it. In the white-on-white living room *opposite,* beige or neutral elements add VITAL WARMING TONES, and the fine touches of black in the metal table, pillow edging, and fireplace art ground the scheme and keep that cloud from floating away. Even the upholstered chair is sheathed in a white and near-white pattern that's so subtle it's hard to notice.

WaTeR COLORS—the cool shades of blue and green—evoke a soothing mood in these two living rooms. And when combined with white, each color shows to its best advantage. In this blue room, pattern is evident but restrained to keep it from disrupting the room's calm. **more contrast** appears *opposite*, where several patterns come into play and the addition of natural wicker and wood gives this room scheme a bit more vibrancy. Accessories, while more abundant than in the blue room, are in a limited range of colors to maintain the room's tranquillity.

"cool, cozy and calm."

bottom. But know yourself well before you try this. Many people find a dark, cavelike room more depressing than relaxing.

ORDER is the order of the day for a serene setting. I can't feel calm, tranquil, and at peace if I'm surrounded by a smothering bunch of "stuff." Too much furniture, too many accessories, everything arranged (or disarranged) helter-skelter, and I can feel my

ORDER BEGETS SERENITY and it's the quiet, undisturbed sense of order that gives these rooms their tranquillity. In each case, the furniture and its arrangement create a stabilizing, placid feeling. In the bedroom, *opposite*, the Shaker-style four-poster bed with its handsome geometry fills the space and leaves no room for clutter. The living room, *below*, is tidy, restrained, and relies on symmetry for its sense of order—symmetry in the fireplace and mantel arrangement and in the arrangement on the coffee table. The placement of the coffee table, centered on the fireplace, creates a more orderly and serene room arrangement than if it were askew.

blood pressure creeping up. So in creating a room designed for serenity, be selective about furnishings. A few larger accessories will be more pacifying than an overabundance of small items that could result in visual busy-ness. You'll also find that symmetrical or balanced arrangements have an innate tranquillity that asymmetrical arrangements lack.

A good rule of thumb in assembling these arrangements is to work within the lines of an invisible triangle. For a symmetrically balanced arrangement, place the items equally on either side of the imaginary center line. In asymmetrical arrangements, envision the vertical line moving off-center and arrange the accessories on either side of it. In a balanced arrangement, objects don't have to be identical on each side, but they do need to have the same mass and visual weight in order to create an eye-pleasing effect.

Maybe your quiet place isn't surrounded by four walls at all. Maybe it's a porch, a deck, or a spot in your garden.

EQUANIMITY rules in this quiet country dining room, *opposite,* even with a bright red wall and an oriental rug. It's the simplicity of the furniture choices and their arrangement that keep this area calm—and calming. The straight-lined pine table, centered under the slim candle chandelier, starts the order of things. Add a wall piece on either side of the window, a simple runner on the table, and only a few good-sized accessories and the room takes on the visual stability needed for serenity. EVERYDAY ELEMENTS a bowl of shells, blue bottles, roadside flowers, *above*—are grouped to lead the eye in a calming circular path for a restful focal point.

MOTHER NATURE, when showing the docile side of her personality, can soothe your soul the way few things can. Trickling water, the soft sound of birds, and the rustling of leaves are as good as any mantra to wash away tension.

In locating your daydreaming spot, be sure to pick someplace away from traffic and everyday work noises. Pick a place that feels protected and that has something beautiful to look at—a flowering shrub, an interesting old tree, a water

nature has its own tranquilizing effect. The oceanside front porch *below left* is calmed by the basically white decorating scheme as well as by the water and sea air. What could be more peaceful, *below right,* than being rocked by the breezes without being caught in a shower? Put heavy-duty hooks through the siding and a column of the porch and you're in business. The bedroom *opposite* sure beats a sleeping bag for comfort outdoors. Set up a bed on your screened porch, run an extension cord for a floor lamp, and don't exclude some accents for gracious living.

"Let nature surround you and calm you."

garden. And provide yourself with some sweet sounds—bird songs, bubbling water, or even squirrels chattering in the trees overhead. Put yourself where you can see and enjoy nature and let it surround and calm you.

CREATURE COMFORTS can give you serenity on a whole other plane of existence. Shed your weary self along with your clothes and slip into a warm, scented bath. Or bubble your troubles away in a spa—indoors or out. Add aromatherapy candles and soft music, and your world is transformed.

Serenity is attainable! Why not step off the treadmill and sit down for a few minutes? Make a list of the things that relax you, comfort you, and make you forget the daily demands. Think of favorite colors that calm you and small but special pampering things such as candles or a few flowers in a vase. List the favorite chair, chaise, sofa, or hammock that lets your body really unwind and totally relax.

Then combine as many of these elements as you can, even if it's in a small area. When you've established your peaceful place, it's time to close out the world and, for a few minutes or a few hours, relax and pull your daydreams in around you. That's serenity!

RELAX YOUR BODY and your mind relaxes too. While most of us don't start with a bath as spacious and hedonistic as the one *opposite,* there are things you can emulate, such as a bigger window. No view? Install glass blocks to flood your bath with light. A window seat is wonderful, but if you can't build one in, bring in a bench or chair. Replace your standard tub with a jetted model. And don't forget the aromatherapy candles. STRETCH OUT. Any chaise or lounger, *above,* gives you an opportunity to relax. This comfy chaise takes on even more softness (and good looks) with the addition of a luxurious cushion covered in a quiet, restful pattern.

SECURITY
SIMPLICITY
WHIMSY
HAPPINESS
ROMANCE
SERENITY

COMFORT

ESCAPES
ENRICHMENT
CELEBRATION

COMFORT

To truly appreciate comfort, just think back to some of your most *un*comfortable moments—physical and emotional. When I do that, I'm remembering three hours on a sunny Sunday afternoon that helped me sort out how I viewed comfort and discomfort in relation to people, houses—and myself.

It happened during my freshman year of college. I was rushed by a sorority and invited to a tea at the home of one of its members. The house was spectacular—one of the big, old mansions in the city's most moneyed residential area. Being a less-than-moneyed design

student, I was impressed. Then at the door my impression changed! The interior was as cold as its stone exterior and everything—furnishings, food, even the hostess—seemed as unapproachable and unfriendly as a crime scene. I was miserable.

The experience made me think of my own family's home—how unpretentious it was, yet how warm and livable. We never owned a chair that couldn't be sat on, either because its covering had to be protected or because it was just plain uncomfortable. And we never served food that guests couldn't even identify! Neither our home nor the way we lived could have been considered classy, but no one could ever argue that it wasn't comfortable and welcoming. And personally, I'd trade class for comfort any day.

The national survey that revealed Americans' desire for security also showed that their preference for comfort is high on the list and increasing. I've read all the statistics—how more people are wearing jeans, doing more informal at-home entertaining, etc. But then, no one had to convince me. I've been a believer for years.

PAGE 145: real comfort, both physical and emotional, is palpable in a room like this one. The chairs are pillowed, the gateleg side table is close by, and there's an ottoman for your feet. The warmth of the pine table and natural wicker chairs gives the room its inviting character, while whimsy comes from the combination of six different patterns—all blue and white to keep them compatible. For a breezy look, try a cafe curtain skimming across a casement window. wicker relaxes the room *opposite*. The sofa is cushioned, pillowed, and draped with a quilt all devices for comfort. To create visual impact, recruit art. Here a large watercolor dominates the wall between windows, creating an eye-high point of interest. The painting's wide white mat echoes the window trim to tie the area together.

"THE GOAL a room THAT IS AS FRIENDLY as a TAIL-WAGGIN' PUPPY and as COMFY as a BIG T-SHIRT."

There are four different aspects to making a room and its occupants comfortable. The first is physical. We all understand comfort for our bodies (sitting, lying, etc.). But if a room is hard to maintain, it can't be considered totally comfortable. Here's the place for slipcovers, washable fabrics, and no-hassle floors.

"Physical" is one aspect of comfort, but to be truly comfortable, a room also has to offer you visual comfort (friendly and easy to look at), emotional comfort (familiar and inviting), and financial comfort (affordable). Comfort is less a decorating style, more a lifestyle, and the key words for creating a room that fits you like your favorite jeans are informal, unpretentious, relaxed, and easygoing. To slip into this decorating style, here are the tools you'll need.

COLOR is an easy way into comfort. Pick any hue on the color wheel and it can yield a

everyone (PETS INCLUDED) is welcome in this easygoing family room. To put out the welcome sign in your home, choose durable fabrics for upholstery or slipcovers and a floor as easy to keep clean as this sisal rug and hardwood flooring. Opt for country wood pieces, with their already aged finishes; hard use will only add to their patina.

comfortable room—as long as you like it. A couple of basic tips: In making a color choice, consider the room's visual temperature. If it's a sunny room given to hot flashes, maybe you'd like to color it cool. A room with naturally cool north light may call for a toastier hue (particularly if you live where your winter view includes snow and ice).

PATTERN choices for this kind of unassuming, lived-in room include plaids, checks, stripes, country prints, small-scale floral prints, and the designs of vintage fabrics. And speaking of fabrics, here's where you can use informal weaves such as gingham, muslin, or canvas, as well as casual fabric surfaces such as chintz or polished cotton.

FURNITURE needs to be—what else?—comfortable. Seating pieces should be soft, with sink-into upholstery or cushions and backed with pillows for even more comfort. Storage pieces need to be practical, but they'll also help create the comfortable look if they have some age—a hutch or buffet that could have stored great-granny's everyday dishes, for example. Furniture surfaces can show wear (I like to think of it as showing love) and favorite woods, such as pine or cherry, are light and warm. Painted, distressed, or crackle finishes also fit nicely into the comfort picture.

Wicker and rattan are big favorites for this look, probably because they signal leisure and

QUILTS EVOKE WARMTH whether on a bed or a wall. In the bedroom *above*, the wall quilt features a strong graphic design that's almost contemporary. If you like bold colors and geometric shapes, explore Amish quilts. They're perfect for sleek modern interiors. In the living room *opposite*, the quilt is the starting point for the room's color scheme. Pick colors from the quilt design to interpret in other fabrics, accessories, even your wall color. Another tip: This quilt is ideally placed on the window wall so sunlight won't harm it.

"LITTLE LUXURIES

are LIFE'S comforts. "

HOW'S THIS for your own B&B—bed and bath? This cleverly designed master suite in an old farmhouse features an elevated bath at one end of the room. By raising the floor in the bath area and hanging a partial curtain, the space looks set apart even though it's not. The bookcase divider also adds to the area's semi-privacy. In the bedroom, a taller-than-average lamp sits on a low bench to put the light at exactly the right height for reading in bed.

relaxation. No one ever sat nervously on the edge of a wicker chair wringing her hands in anxiety. Now the furniture that once was relegated to porches or summer houses has crept comfortably into interiors and brought along its relaxed, casual look.

Part of the beauty of a homey, easygoing look is that it can be pulled off on a skimpy budget. Garage sale and flea market treasures fit just fine. As a matter of fact, it's the brand-spanking-shiny-new furniture from a high-end designer showroom that might look out of place.

And remember, while adding comfort to a room, furniture also should add convenience—which, in its own way, is comfort. Chairs should have ottomans so you can put your feet up. Seating areas should be teamed with side tables or a coffee table, so you have a close-at-hand place for your coffee cup, book, or TV remote.

WINDOWS are most comfortable if they're casually dressed. Simple cafe curtains, valances, shades, shutters—they all have the down-to-earth, everyday look you're striving for. Almost anything understated will work at your windows. Just avoid overly fussy or fancy window treatments. In other words, think sport clothes, not dress clothes.

ACCESSORIES are the fun, the life, the personality in your take-off-your-shoes-and-sit-a-spell room. The secret is to include things you like best, and the very best things will have

RELY ON FABRIC to give your dining room a soft, inviting look that bespeaks comfort. Pure white fabric dresses and softens this formal dining room, *above.* To take the hard edge off chairs, slipcover them; to tame a wall of windows, sheathe them in Roman shades. The BLUE AND WHITE dining area *opposite* lavishes fabric on the table, chairs, and window. Balloon shades dress the window with a light, puffy topper, and big bow ties on the chair cushions give even wooden chairs a soft look.

KITCHEN COMFORT comes from having everything you need when you want it—where you want it. And sometimes it comes from simply having a cheery, attractive place to cook. These three kitchens have plenty of ideas for both. Turn a CHEST OF DRAWERS into a kitchen island, *left*. Replace the top with marble for a baker-friendly surface and add towel bars to the sides. For cabinet re-dos, replace solid doors on upper cabinets with glass-pane ones. Under the sink, take doors off completely and replace them with a shirred curtain to create a vintage look. Want something MORE FUN than a standard island? Bring in an old farm table, *center*. It adds a spacious work/serving surface, roomy storage drawers, and the warmth of pine. With everything in the kitchen white—including the brick chimney

in the corner—the wood of the table creates a honey-toned focal point. The kitchen, *right,* has reinforced its 1920s CHaracter with a new farmhouse-style single-bowl sink reminiscent of the old wall-hung porcelain variety. To add even more vintage character, car siding surfaces the walls and open shelves span a corner that's too small for a cabinet. The pass-through to the dining room was part of the original architecture, but molding was added to match that of the windows. A unifying idea for any home is the slim molding that skips along the top of the window frames. In the kitchen the wall is painted the same color above and below the accent strip, but in the adjacent dining room the area above it changes color to lift the eye and add interest.

been with you for a while. Include treasures that have been passed down from family members; interesting, quirky objects you fell in love with at a flea market; things the kids made at camp or that you picked up on vacation.

In this kind of unfussy, serviceable room, it's also nice to have accessories that are usable. Pitchers are great on shelves, even better when they hold bouquets of garden flowers. And the

clock that was your father's is worth more emotionally than the price you'll pay to have it repaired. So get it fixed and running. You'll think of Dad every time the chime sounds—and there's real comfort in that!

Comfort isn't only how soft the cushion is that you sit on. It's how warm your heart feels when you're surrounded by colors, patterns, and pieces of your past that really please you.

PORCHES AND COMFORT are synonymous. The crisp blue and white porch *below* is a swingin' (and rockin') place with not a stationary seat in sight. And just for fun, plant a window box on the porch railing. The porch *opposite* turns the OUTSIDE INSIDE. To do the same, hang a curtain rod and drape a curtain panel between the window's shutters. The harlequin-patterned painted floor is another creative, easy-to-do idea for an interior look.

SECURITY
SIMPLICITY
WHIMSY
HAPPINESS
romance
serenity
comfort

escapes

enrichment
CELEBRATION

escapes

Every once in a while, even the most responsible of us feels the urge to dump everything and run away. Though we don't need to go to Thoreau's extreme (a packing crate on Walden Pond might seem a bit excessive even in today's world), his philosophy still speaks to us and is TIMELESS. All of us can benefit from having a tiny corner, a quiet room, or a spot in the yard where we can GET AWAY TO DAYDREAM, RECHARGE–OR JUST "BE."

The first time I experienced the thrill of a getaway was when I was about six or seven. At that age I was too young to need recharging,

certainly, but I was too much of a daydreamer to want to stay constantly plugged into the all-in-the-family thing. Then, without realizing it, Dad created my first "escape." He built me a playhouse, complete with window and window box, and immediately it became MY OWN PRIVATE WORLD. I played there, sure. I cooked imaginary meals and had conversations with imaginary friends. But most of my hours were spent poring over an old Montgomery Ward catalog and LETTING MY MIND WANDER as my fingers turned the dog-eared pages filled with photos of toys, furniture, and "fancy lady" clothes.

Long after my playhouse days have become treasured childhood memories, I still long for some TINY, QUIET PLACE to "be." Once you've tasted the restorative peacefulness of your own escape, you never want to be without it. And a special spot really is not hard to create. It can be small and simply furnished as long as it's private and NURTURES the dream-spinner in you.

At my current home my escape is a sliver of patio space beside the house (page 29). It's here I sip coffee, read the paper, and soak up the fresh smells and quiet sounds of early morning. It's perfect! And I love it—even without a Ward's catalog.

PAGE 163: IT'S HEAVENLY to walk down a sun-dappled garden path like this one. While the path always is beautiful, it's truly spectacular in summer when it's lined with majestic fuchsia and white phlox. To add fluttering friends to your walk, plant perennials that attract butterflies—coneflower, bee balm, or butterfly bushes. When you want to run away and hide, a COZY WINDOW ALCOVE, opposite, is perfect. It has everything—shelves for favorite books, a pull-up bench to hold your tea, and a cushioned and pillow-filled spot for relaxing. No window alcove? Create a snug nest in a dormer or a bay window flanked by freestanding bookcases.

" THE GOAL a quiet place to dream dreams and feel they'll come true. **"**

Want to get away? You can! Creating your escape starts with finding the right spot.

LOCATION is everything (as any real estate agent is quick to tell you) whether you're buying a house or hunting for the perfect getaway in or around the home you live in. Chances are your instinct will tell you when a place feels right to you—a place that feels inviting, protective, and freeing. But there are some other more tangible criteria to consider too.

The first should be locating a spot that's "away" but not isolated. An out-of-the way nook in a bedroom, on a porch, or close by in the yard gives you the privacy you're looking for yet still keeps you within easy commuting distance of the "convenience areas" of your home—for me, the kitchen and the bathroom. Spots that hold greatest appeal as escapes include a dormer in a bedroom, an alcove on a landing, a built-in window bench in the living room—any place that offers a tucked-away, private feeling.

If you have your eye on a more remote spot—a shady area in the far corner of your yard or possibly a separate outdoor structure—there are some big advantages to that kind of location too. An escape that's physically removed from your home gives you even more privacy and lets you

HIDING OUT in this upstairs bedroom is easy. Everything about it wraps you in tranquillity, from the protective-feeling wingback chair and fluffy-as-a-cloud bed dressings to the enchanting dormer alcove. This tiny space, used here as a desk area, would work just as well as a reading room, pint-size study, or studio for painting. The trick is small-scale furniture and a window treatment that doesn't eat up space.

do your reading, thinking, or daydreaming without disruption from the phone or doorbell.

Look for a place that appeals to you emotionally and gives you a feeling of freedom from your day-to-day routine. Some spots will, others won't. For instance, a chair nestled in a clump of trees will give you a lot more freedom, both emotionally and mentally, than would the same chair in the corner of a basement laundry room, no matter how comfortable it was or how far removed physically from household hustle and bustle. The laundry still represents the work you're escaping. Also avoid any high-traffic areas or places where the whole family gathers. Even if

a screen porch like the one *above* offers folksy enchantment, from its painted floor to the ornate screen doors. The snug little living area, *opposite,* occupies one end of an open porch. In addition to the hammock, there's a tight little grouping of furniture, including a pair of rockers and a love seat. If hammocks don't appeal to you, you can still enjoy subtle motion with a glider or porch swing. Keep colors fresh and outdoorsy for a sunny effect.

"a peaceful, calm feeling."

DINING ALFRESCO is paradise for two in the semisheltered courtyard *opposite*. Brick surrounded by a redwood fence defines the living area; beyond that, low creeping ground cover, high towering climbers, and a mix of flowering shrubs and perennials create living walls. If your courtyard is too small for a redwood dining set, plan to use less massive furniture—wrought iron or wicker. **SLIP AWAY** for a quiet hour in a shaded, covered deck. The garden beyond is a mix of shaped hedges, perennials, and annuals. To bring the garden closer, load the deck with pots of blooming plants.

you're alone physically, you can't *feel* alone in a room that's normally a busy activity center.

AMBIENCE is the second consideration. The spot you choose should be quiet, coddling you with pleasant surroundings—a view or at least something attractive to look at while you're daydreaming. Lighting should be soft and, if you're outside, filtered through leafy foliage.

FURNISHINGS for your getaway don't need to be fancy. What you're creating is a place where you can lose yourself for a little while. It doesn't matter if the chair you sit in is fresh from the showroom floor or reclaimed from the attic, just as long as it's comfortable. Some of the all-time favorite furniture pieces for spaces like this are rockers, hammocks, and big, soft upholstered chairs that invite you to sit down and curl up. Choose casual fabrics with colors and patterns that are easy to live with (both visually and physically). And for the finishing touch of comfort, nothing beats plenty of pillows. They can plump up any piece of furniture and make it as soft as a kitten—and just as inviting.

EXTRAS. You don't need a lot of paraphernalia when you're escaping. Travel light! Be sure to include a few of your favorite things— a piece of art you particularly enjoy looking at, your best-loved books, or the music you like. This is your own private world so give it your

WHAT LOOKS LIKE THE SERENGETI, *opposite,* is really a Midwestern farm field given some glamour. Any portable tent can look as glamorous when swagged and draped with gauze, then banked with potted ferns. Bring out a table and chairs, string some lamps, and let the party begin. For an evening affair, use citronella candles in the lamps to keep mosquitoes at bay. A MINI GAZEBO? An arbor with a bench? Call it what you will, this charming garden structure, *above,* can be your perfect hideaway. Plans for similar units are available from building-supply stores, but a good builder can duplicate this one by studying the photo. Plant vines, clematis, or climbing roses to meander up the lattice, giving you a snug, cozy feeling, as well as the best kind of aromatherapy.

personal stamp. If you like, bring some pleasant time-passers too—a sketch pad, a book or magazine, or writing material. Something to drink or nibble is often welcome, but resist plugging in a coffeepot. It's apt to be followed by a minirefrigerator and then, next thing you know, you'll have equipped a satellite kitchen. I don't know about you, but that's hardly my idea of "escape."

Probably the best inspiration for carving out a quiet spot of your own are the words of a woman whose home we photographed for *Better Homes and Gardens* magazine. She told us, "I find many reasons besides sleeping to be in my bedroom. I love to sit in my grandmother's wing chair and simply listen to the rustle of leaves outside the window."

There you have it—the formula for a perfect escape: feather-soft seating or snoozing places that envelop you with physical comfort, a touch of tradition or heritage that links you with a past worth contemplating, and nature—a companion that constantly soothes and entertains you without interrupting your solace.

PreTTY SOPHISTICATeD camping out, I'd say. The secluded retreat, *above*, can be duplicated by building a wall of screened openings in an unused garage or outbuilding. Cover the screens with a sheet hung by shower rings on cup hooks or use curtains hung from tension rods. anOTHer SaLVaGe JOB—this time an old shed converted to an "escape." A coat of paint on the walls, ceiling, and floor and it's ready to be furnished. Use painted primitive furniture, quilts, and vintage fabric to create a relaxed, used-before look— perfect for a serene escape.

WOODLAND FAIRIES—or at the very least, Little Red Riding Hood—might be expected to join you in this iris grove sanctuary, *opposite*. Just take a chair (or two) out into the farthest reaches of your garden and escape into nature. Wood chairs will weather to a soft, warm patina. MEDITATION or recreation—the wooded hideaway, *center*, can handle either. If your style isn't weathered wood, use vinyl. A big advantage to vinyl chairs is that they stack and are light enough to carry back to the deck or patio. In the OUTDOOR ROOM, *right*, old-fashioned folding deck chairs have come ashore to join the enticing hammock. With the addition of a couple of tables, you have a real, honest-to-goodness living room. The first challenge in creating your own pastoral parlor is to find two shade trees spaced so they'll support the hammock. Then add the mix of furniture you want. Even accessories are welcome. For an evening retreat, illuminate the area with candles on the table and lanterns in the trees.

FOCUS ON FLOWERS

NANTUCKET ISLAND
ROBERT GAMBEE

AMERICAN BORDER GARDENS

FLOWERS REDISCOVERED REVISED EDITION

THE ILLUSTRATED GERTRUDE JEKYLL

ICONS OF THE 20TH CENTURY

GARDENING WITH ROSES   McKEON

Landscaping With Perennials   Emily Brown

beds and borders

SEASIDE GARDENING

GARDENING with HERBS

SECURITY
SIMPLICITY
WHIMSY
HAPPINESS
romance
serenity
comfort
escapes
enrichment
celebration

enrichment

My mother has told me (repeatedly, I might add) that as a youngster I had the attention span of a flea. And very much like a flea, I flitted from one thing to another. I never was challenged for long, always **searching** for something more, something new to look at, read, or do. But then, how could I help being a "flea?" Our whole family functioned that way—first the **challenge**, then **exploration**, **fulfillment**, **enrichment**—then another challenge. Mom was challenged by the next short story she'd write, while Dad was challenged building our house, board by board. And my brother, a

mechanical engineer in the making, was challenged by anything and everything he could take apart and put back together. Each of us was busy doing, learning, growing.

I realize now that being raised in a family like mine **ENRICHED** my life in ways that I didn't understand at the time and that continue to influence me even today. When I browse a bookstore, for instance, a phrase from the past echoes in my head: "Don't just read. Read something good." And at a concert: "If you're going to have lessons, piano would give you a basic understanding of music." (What I really wanted to learn was tap dancing!) Thanks to my family, I grew up with a **DEEP APPRECIATION** of the arts, an inquiring nature, and a feeling of satisfaction every time I learned something new. And I'd bet the last penny in my book budget that I'm not at all different from the people whose homes or studios you'll see in this chapter. We're all searching for enrichment—**DELVING DEEPER** into our interests, hobbies, or at-home professions.

I'd also bet I wasn't the only kid whose parents' biggest challenge was keeping us challenged. In our own ways, we were all "fleas." Many of us still are.

PAGE 181: **A DESK FOR TWO** by day, a buffet by night. All it takes to create the double desk is a long table with a shorter one placed perpendicular to it. Desktop office trappings are housed in attractive baskets, then stashed on the lower shelf when it's party time. For a less contemporary look, hang a quilt behind the table and keep office supplies in crates or wood-burned boxes. **AN OLD GARDEN SHED,** *opposite,* has been given a second life as a sewing center and getaway, thanks to a paint job and a sisal rug. The quilt rack displays vintage tablecloths, but it also could hold folded yardages of sewing fabric.

THE GOAL a room that's
want it to be—so you
of what you

You should know right up front that what you're looking at in this chapter are "dream spaces." They probably don't bear much resemblance to the corners in which we currently paint or quilt or listen to music. For most of us, enriching our lives through our hobbies (or businesses) happens in a shared space—either in a dual-function room or, as in the case of my painting, in a few square feet of a general-purpose room (pages 20 and 23). The good thing about any enrichment area, no matter how small, is that we've set one up and we're enjoying it. But the really, really good thing about an area like those shown here is that you don't have to clean up your mess or put away your tools before the family comes home.

Most enrichment areas have the same requirements—they need a work surface, storage space, and good light. Granted, some need a few more amenities (such as comfortable seating in a media center); however, the bare-bone necessities are similar and simple. The spaces on these pages go way beyond bare bones. They're inspirational, aspirational, and jam-packed with ideas for "extras"—those specialized features you can adapt for your own home—the stuff dreams are made of.

ONE HALF OF A GARAGE equals a whole studio. Here a wall of windows replaced the door and pavers finished the floor. Studio furniture should be kept light in scale and leggy to avoid blocking sunlight. Ration pattern and wall art to avoid distractions, but pin up things that feed your eye—postcards, snapshots, fabric swatches that inspire you.

everything you can be more want to be. "

PAINTING doesn't get much better than in the studio on these and the preceding pages! I'd give up a whole lot of luxuries in life to have a painting space where I could both escape and create. But paradise aside, the basics you need include enough space for your easel to allow you to stand back and view your work, a close-at-hand surface for paints and brushes, and good light. The "dream" thing—the element that would make a painting studio perfect—would be attractive, stimulating surroundings, both inside and out. It can't help but inspire you and get your creative juices flowing.

WOODWORKING can be a real space-

NOT AN INCH of this studio is wasted. In the back corner, a ladder (chosen over a stairway because of its rustic character) goes up to a storage loft, *right*. Beyond the ladder is a charming sitting room, *opposite*—a perfect place to unwind and consider works in progress or finished pieces. Here's where you'll find the pattern and wall art that are absent in the painting area. Art often can be as captivating unframed as framed. To hang unframed watercolors without damaging them, use clips attached to the wall.

room to craft

gobbling pursuit, depending on what you build. Furniture builders, obviously, require more storage space for materials than birdhouse builders do. But the dream of every woodworker is plenty of floor space for power tools, drawer space to keep even the smallest items organized, and wall space to keep frequently used items close at hand.

For both home builders and the quilting and stitching crowd, the necessities are: plenty of

a project
or a dream."

HERE'S A WOOD SHOP TO WISH FOR. This addition to the back of a garage provides plenty of floor space for tools, work tables, and projects in process. One of the unique features is the roll-around tool pyramid, designed and built by the wood shop owner to keep tools handy. You could create something similar by attaching a piece of Peg Board to a sturdy artist's easel on casters. Since space always is at a premium, this builder designed his drafting table to roll under the workbench when the table isn't in use.

power outlets, good light (both overall lighting and task lighting), and surfaces that are easy to sweep or vacuum.

Ask any fabric crafter: She'll tell you her dream would be a wall full of cubbyholes or shelves to store folded fabrics in full view and a big cutting table that floats in enough space to allow work from all four sides.

HOME OFFICES need more flat surfaces

QUILTING may be the world's most addictive craft. And once you're hooked, any piece of fabric you think you might ever use comes home with you. In the sewing center, *opposite* and *below*, fabrics are arranged on open shelves according to color. If you don't have built-in shelves, you can use ready-made storage shelf units or stack clear plastic boxes on a table. The quilter's sewing table, *below*, was custom-made with a lowered surface for the machine. You can get the same effect by placing your sewing machine on the pull-out keyboard shelf of a home office computer unit. Just check the sturdiness of the shelf against the weight of your machine.

a PLAN WITH a PLACE

FEW THINGS RECALL the past like bits of nostalgia that take you back to Mom's kitchen or Grandma's porch. The kitchen *opposite* certainly smacks of another time. Unusually high beaded-board wainscoting, vintage fabrics, crockery, and enamelware all add to the room's nostalgia. The porch scene *below left* could be an early 1900s luncheon table set with square chintzware. Using the matching pitcher filled with lush flowers is just the right finishing touch. Vintage handkerchiefs form a table runner in this kitchen, *below right*. You don't even need to sew them; simply layer them on the table and anchor at least one with a fruit bowl or vase of flowers.

celebrating TIMES PAST.

HAPPINESS DOESN'T ALWAYS COME from expensive things. It can come, just as easily, from enjoying the gifts of nature, the beauty of craftsmanship, or the pleasure of your home. Spring makes an early entrance on this windowsill, *below left*. Even cold late-winter rains can't dampen your spirits with these happy little irises around. For spring blooms, you can winter bulbs in the refrigerator or buy them at a garden center precooled and ready to force into bloom. Nestle the bulbs in decorative rocks and grow them in water. An arrangement of exquisitely crafted baskets, *center*, brings beauty and order to this window ledge. Add greenery for contrast. Breezes are nature's special gift. Wafting in through a sheer curtain, *opposite*, the breeze is tranquilizing, just slightly ethereal, and definitely something to celebrate. When you think about it, it's really the simple things in life that can bring us happiness—if we only take time to appreciate them.

"celebrating simple joys."

RESOURCES & ACKNOWLEDGMENTS
Portrait photos, pages 25, 31, and 205
right, Andy Lyons. Photographs on pages
17–27, 29–31, and 210, Hopkins Associates;
stylist, Joseph Boehm. Photograph on page 9,
Photonica; page 10 Magnus Rietz/Photonica;
page 15 Robert Mizono/Workbook Stock.
Except as noted, photography courtesy
of *Better Homes and Gardens*® magazine
and *Country Home*® magazine.